59372083673726   FIG

Ryan Howard

Revised Edition

By Jeff Savage

NOT
AMAZING
ATHLETES

Lerner Publications Company • Minneapolis

Lerner Publications Company
A division of Lerner Publishing Group, Inc.
241 First Avenue North
Minneapolis, MN 55401 U.S.A.

Website address: www.lernerbooks.com

Library of Congress Cataloging-in-Publication Data

Savage, Jeff, 1961–
    Ryan Howard / by Jeff Savage. — Rev. ed.
        p.   cm. — (Amazing athletes)
    Includes index.
    ISBN: 978–0–7613–8669–8 (lib. bdg. : alk. paper)
    1. Howard, Ryan, 1979– —Juvenile literature. 2. Baseball players—United States—Biography—Juvenile literature. I. Title.
    GV865.H67S38 2012
    796.357092—dc23 [B]   2011036054

Manufactured in the United States of America
1 – BP – 12/31/11

TABLE OF CONTENTS

Fans packed the stands at Citizens Bank Park in Philadelphia, Pennsylvania.

BIG MOMENT

Ryan Howard stepped into the **batter's box**. The Philadelphia Phillies' first baseman gripped his bat and pointed it at the pitcher. The crowd at Citizens Bank Park in Philadelphia, Pennsylvania, roared around him.

Ryan and the Phillies were playing the St. Louis Cardinals in the first game of the 2011 **National League Division Series (NLDS)**. Philadelphia's **ace pitcher** Roy Halladay started the game. But Halladay had given up a three-run home run to the Cardinals in the first inning. "I couldn't think of a worse start than putting your team in a hole like that," Halladay said later. The Phillies needed Ryan to help them get back in the game.

Roy Halladay winds up for a pitch.

When Ryan came to bat in the sixth inning, the Cardinals had the lead, 3–1. Teammates Jimmy Rollins and Hunter Pence were on base. Ryan knew that this was his big moment to help the team.

Cardinals pitcher Kyle Lohse threw a **changeup** to Ryan. Then he threw three more changeups. When Lohse threw his fifth changeup, Ryan swung and sent the ball high into the night sky. It cleared the wall in right field for a home run! Ryan's swing gave Philadelphia a 4–3 lead. "I knew he wasn't really going to throw a **fastball**, so I just sat on the changeup," Ryan said after the game.

The Phillies scored more runs in the seventh and eighth innings and won the game, 11–6. Ryan was glad to have helped his team win this important game.

Ryan swings for a three-run home run in the sixth inning.

Ryan's teammate Raul Ibanez was not surprised that the big first baseman had come through when his team needed him most. "That's what he does," Ibanez said. "You watch him do it all the time."

Ryan was born in Saint Louis, Missouri, home of the famous Gateway Arch.

A PLAYFUL BOY

Ryan James Howard was born November 19, 1979, in Saint Louis, Missouri. Ryan's parents, Ron and Cheryl, taught their children to be confident. They told their kids to never use the word *can't*. Ryan's twin brother, Corey; older brother, Chris; and sister, Roni, all did well in school.

Ryan was a big, playful boy. He liked to tell jokes and had lots of friends at school. But he was serious when it was time for schoolwork. His favorite subject was history.

Ryan's favorite sport was baseball. As a big, strong left-hander, he was a natural to play first base. His nickname was Hurt because he hit the ball so hard. "When he made contact, it was like, 'Wow!'" said his brother Corey. "His home runs were loud."

By the age of 12, Ryan had become a monster batter at the plate. In one Little League game, he bashed a ball way over the fence. It sailed so far that it landed on the roof of a restaurant 430 feet away. "That ball was flying," said Cheryl. "That was one of the first times I thought he could be a **major leaguer** one day."

Ryan played football on this field at Lafayette High School in Missouri.

Ryan enjoyed a fun, busy life at Lafayette High School. In the fall, he played on the football team. He also played the trombone in the marching band. Practicing both was not easy. Most days, Ryan ran straight from the football field to band practice nearby. "He would

Ryan has several nicknames. Here are some of them: Powered Howard, Rhino, Man-Mountain, One-Man Gang.

throw his shoulder pads to the side and play the trombone in his cleats," said Phil Milligan, the school's band director.

In the winter, Ryan played on the basketball team. He gobbled up rebounds and blocked shots. In the spring came his favorite sport— baseball. He set a school record with 17 career home runs. His powerful swings became legendary. Once he bashed a ball so hard that it ripped the glove off an outfielder's hand.

Ryan looked as if he had the hitting skills to be a professional baseball player. But another part of Ryan's game needed to get better.

Ryan always tries to do his best. "I try to be as close to perfect as I can," he says. "You can never reach perfection, but you can still strive for it."

Ryan catches a foul ball in 2004. As a young player, Ryan had to work hard on his fielding.

HARD AT WORK

Throughout high school, Ryan struggled with his **fielding**. This might be the reason why major-league **scouts** chose not to **draft** him for their teams. Colleges weren't interested in him, either.

Ryan's high school coach, Steve Miller, couldn't believe it. He called coach Keith Guttin at nearby Southwest Missouri State University. "Someone is missing the boat with this kid," Miller said. Guttin decided to give Ryan a chance.

Coach Guttin's decision paid off. Ryan went on to become one of the school's all-time best players. In three college seasons, he smashed 50 home runs!

After his third year, the Phillies selected him in the fifth round of the 2001 draft.

The Phillies drafted Ryan after his third year of college. Ryan did not earn his degree—yet. Ryan plans to return to college to finish what he started. "It's a requirement and an expectation. He understands that," says his father. Ryan will take college classes when he can. And he wants to graduate. "Yep, I know it's something I'm going to have to do. And I will," he says.

Like most players, Ryan began his pro career in the **minor leagues**. He would have to learn and improve. If he was good enough and worked hard enough, he would earn his way to the major leagues.

Ryan did just that. And he did it in less than three seasons. He smashed the ball out of minor-league stadiums around the country.

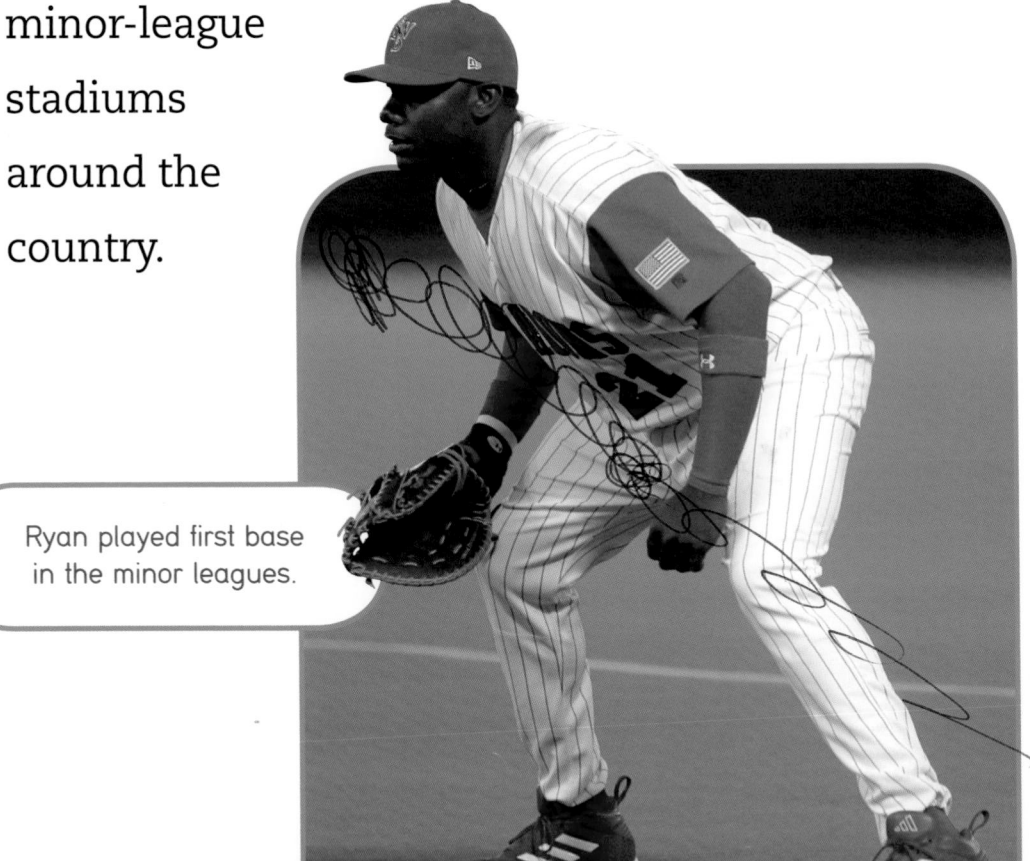

Ryan played first base in the minor leagues.

By late 2004, he was leading the minor leagues with 46 home runs and 131 **runs batted in (RBIs)**. On September 1, the Phillies called him up to the big-league team. Ryan's lifelong dream had come true. He was a Major League Baseball player.

In his first game for the Phillies, he struck out. But soon, he got his first major-league hit. Two days later, he got his first double. Three days after that, he blasted his first big-league home run in an 11–9 win against the New York Mets.

Ryan's career was starting out well. The Phillies and their fans were excited about their talented young first baseman. But there was one problem. The Phillies already had a star first baseman—Jim Thome. Where was Ryan going to play?

Ryan had to work hard to win a place on the Phillies team.

TAKING OVER

As the 2005 season began, the Phillies weren't sure what to do. In spring training, they tried playing Ryan in the outfield. He struggled with fielding. So the team sent him down to the minors.

Ryan was frustrated, but he stayed positive. "We taught Ryan earlier in life that if you keep working hard, eventually you'll get the prize you are seeking," said his father.

One month into the season, Thome hurt his elbow. The Phillies called up Ryan to play first base. In his first game, he smacked three hits in a 4–3 win over the Cincinnati Reds.

Jim Thome plays first base for the Phillies in a game in June 2005. His injury gave Ryan a chance to play.

As the weeks passed, Ryan got some big hits. But he also struck out a lot. At one point in the season, his **batting average** was just .218. "He was trying too hard, over-swinging, and trying to show how good he is," said Phillies manager Charlie Manuel.

Meanwhile, Jim Thome got healthy. When Thome was ready to play, the Phillies sent Ryan back to the minors. No one would have blamed Ryan for being upset. But he did not complain or sulk. Instead, he pounded the ball. He was soon leading his

Ryan has a great attitude. He is gentle and focused. He never seems to get mad. "The only thing that sets him off is hearing people say he can't do things," says his brother Corey. "They've said he can't hit lefties, he can't hit for a high average. Whatever they've said Ryan can't do, he's gone out and done."

league in batting average. His upbeat attitude was paying off.

At the end of June, Thome got hurt again. Ryan was called up on July 1. "We'll bring him up and see what he can do," said Manuel. In Ryan's second game, he blasted a three-run homer against the Atlanta Braves. Soon after, he crushed a game-winning homer to beat the Los Angeles Dodgers. Then he beat the Braves and the Dodgers again with game-winning **grand slams**! "He was completely different when he came back up. More relaxed," said Manuel.

Phillies manager Charlie Manuel watches a 2005 game from the dugout.

Ryan was having fun now. The **rookie** greeted teammates each day with a dozen handshakes. "There's a lot of [strength] in those hands," said teammate Jimmy Rollins.

With Thome out for the rest of the season, Ryan powered the Phillies on an exciting **playoff** chase. He blasted 22 home runs in just 88 games!

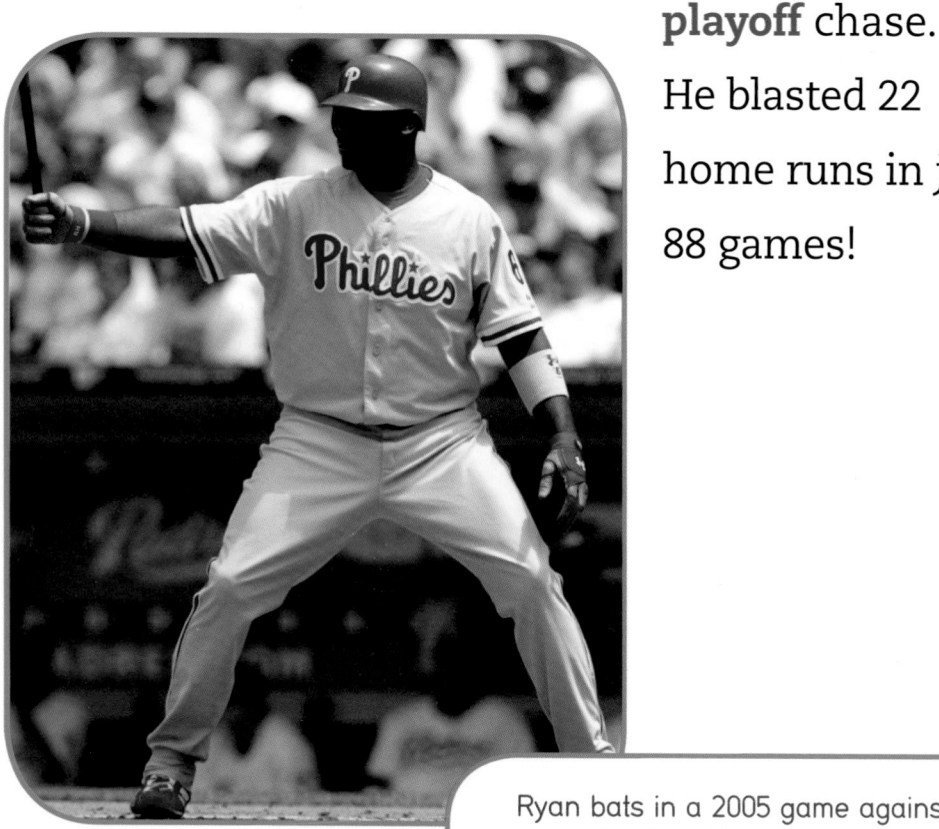

Ryan bats in a 2005 game against the San Diego Padres.

Ryan celebrates after hitting a home run in a September 2005 game.

But the Phillies missed making the playoffs by a single game. "It was a fun run," said Ryan. "We showed a lot of heart, a lot of fight."

After the season, Ryan was named **National League (NL)** Rookie of the Year. "He honestly carried the team," said pitcher Billy Wagner. "I've never seen a kid have such an impact that soon, just come up and really take over a team."

Ryan became the Phillies starting first baseman in 2006.

WORLD CHAMPIONS

Before the start of the 2006 season, the Phillies traded Thome to the Chicago White Sox. First base belonged to Ryan. He was ready. By midseason, he was leading the majors with 30 home runs.

Ryan was voted to the NL team for the 2006 **All-Star Game** in Pittsburgh, Pennsylvania. The day before the game, he competed against some of baseball's best sluggers in the **Home Run Derby**. Ryan hit 23 home runs. He even whacked several balls out of the stadium and into the nearby Allegheny River. Ryan won the derby.

Ryan finished the season with 58 home runs, the most in the major leagues. He also led the majors in RBIs with 149. His amazing stats earned him the 2006 National League **Most Valuable Player (MVP) Award**.

Ryan poses with his trophy after winning the 2006 Home Run Derby.

Phillies fans expected great things from Ryan in 2007. As usual, he led the team with 47 homers and 136 RBIs. The Phillies passed the New York Mets on the final day of the season to reach the playoffs. Philadelphia didn't last long, though. The Colorado Rockies swept them in three straight games.

The Phillies are a much better team when Ryan is playing well.

The 2008 season would be special for Ryan and the Phillies. The big slugger had another great year, smashing 48 home runs with 146 RBIs. Best of all, the Phillies were back in the playoffs. This time the team was ready. Philadelphia beat the Milwaukee Brewers and the Dodgers to reach the World Series.

Ryan keeps his eye on the ball. Ryan's hitting helped the Phillies reach the World Series in 2008.

Philadelphia beat the Tampa Bay Rays in five games in the World Series. The Phillies were world champions! "We're winners," Ryan said. "Nobody can take that away from the city of Philadelphia."

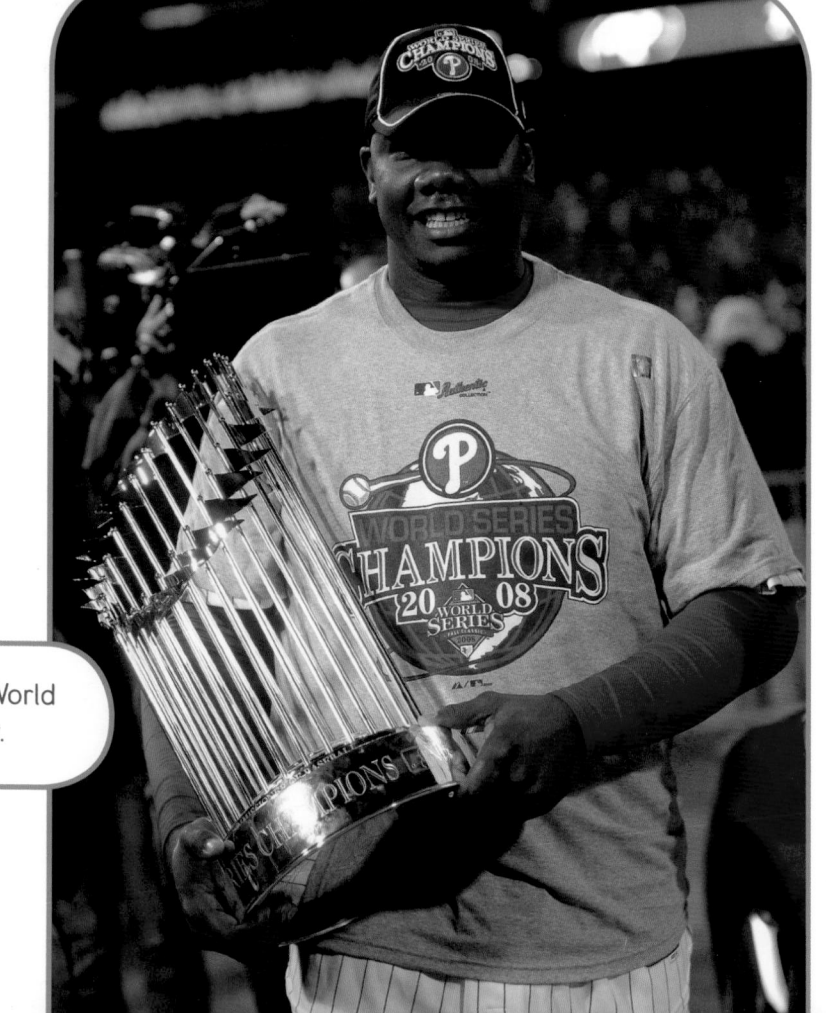

Ryan holds the World Series trophy.

Ryan hits a two-run home run in game six of the 2009 World Series.

Ryan and the Phillies were back in the playoffs in 2009. Once again, they faced the Rockies in the first round. This time, the Phillies came out on top, winning the series in four games. When they beat the Dodgers in the second round, Philadelphia was headed to the World Series for the second year in a row. They lost to the New York Yankees in six games.

Ryan likes to sign autographs for fans.

The Phillies came up short of the World Series in 2010 and 2011. But with Ryan in the lineup, the Phillies have a great chance to be world champions again someday. "I just want to play as hard as I can, be the best I can, and be remembered for that," says Ryan.

Selected Career Highlights

2011 Finished third in the NL in RBIs, with 116
Finished sixth in the NL in home runs, with 33

2010 Finished fourth in the NL in RBIs, with 108

2009 Finished third in the NL in RBIs, with 135
Finished third in the NL in home runs, with 45

2008 Led the Phillies to victory in the World Series
Finished first in the NL in RBIs, with 146
Finished first in the NL in home runs, with 48

2007 Finished second in the NL in home runs, with
47
Finished second in the NL in RBIs, with 136

2006 Won NL Most Valuable Player Award
Led MLB in home runs with 58
Led MLB in runs batted in with 149
Became first Phillies player to hit more than 50 home runs in a
season
Won Home Run Derby at the All-Star Game

2005 Named NL Rookie of the Year
Led MLB rookies with 22 home runs
Broke MLB rookie record for home runs in September with 10

2004 Played in first major-league game for Philadelphia Phillies on
September 1
Led minor leagues with 46 home runs and 131 runs batted in
Named MVP of the Eastern League (minor league) as a member of
the Reading (Pennsylvania) Phillies

2003 Named MVP of the Florida State League (minor league) as a member of
the Clearwater Threshers
Led the Florida State league with a .304 batting average
Led the Florida State league in home runs with 23

2002 Led all Phillies minor leaguers in home runs with 19, while playing
for the Lakewood Blue Claws (New Jersey)
Named to South Atlantic League All-Star team

2001 Selected in the fifth round of the MLB draft

Glossary

ace pitcher: a team's best starting pitcher

All-Star Game: a special game held in July each year between a group of the best major-league players, as voted by fans

batter's box: the rectangular area on each side of home plate in which the batter stands

batting average: a statistic that shows a player's success at hitting the ball. For example, if a hitter gets 3 hits in 10 at-bats, the batting average would be .300.

changeup: a pitch that looks like a fastball coming out of the pitcher's hand but arrives much more slowly

draft: to choose a player for a pro team; also a yearly event in which professional teams take turns choosing new players from a selected group

fastball: a fast pitch that usually travels straight

fielding: catching and throwing the baseball while playing in the field

grand slams: home runs in which there are runners on all the bases. These home runs produce four runs.

Home Run Derby: a contest held every year the night before the All-Star Game. In this contest, a selected group of players compete to see who can hit the most home runs.

major leagues: the top level of professional baseball. Major League Baseball (MLB) is divided into the National League and the American League.

minor leagues: a group of teams where players work to improve their skills and prepare to move to the major leagues

Most Valuable Player (MVP) Award: an award given each year to the player who has been judged to have been the most valuable player to his team that season

National League (NL): one of baseball's two major leagues

National League Division Series (NLDS): a set of games played at the end of the baseball season between two of the top four NL teams. The team that wins three games goes to the Championship Series (NLCS). The winner of the NLCS goes to the World Series to play the winner of the American League Championship Series (ALCS).

playoff: a series of games played to decide which team is the Major League Baseball champion

rookie: a player who is in his or her first season

runs batted in (RBIs): the number of runners able to score on a batter's action, such as a hit or a walk

scouts: people who judge the skills of players. Scouts work for individual teams and help them decide whom to draft.

Further Reading & Websites

Kennedy, Mike, and Mark Stewart. *Long Ball: The Legend and Lore of the Home Run*. Minneapolis: Millbrook Press, 2006.

Patrick, Jean L. S. *The Baseball Adventure of Jackie Mitchell, Girl Pitcher vs. Babe Ruth*. Minneapolis: Graphic Universe, 2011.

Savage, Jeff. *Roy Halladay*. Minneapolis: Lerner Publications Company, 2011.

The Official Site of Major League Baseball
http://www.mlb.com
Major League Baseball's official website provides fans with the latest scores and game schedules, as well as information on players, teams, and baseball history.

Philadelphia Phillies: The Official Site
http://philadelphiaphillies.com
The official website of the Philadelphia Phillies includes the team schedule and game results, late-breaking news, biographies of Ryan Howard and other players and coaches, and much more.

Sports Illustrated Kids
http://www.sikids.com
The *Sports Illustrated Kids* website covers all sports, including baseball.

Index

Photo Acknowledgments

The images in this book are used with the permission of: © Drew Hallowell/Getty Images, p. 4; © Rob Carr/Getty Images, p. 5; AP Photo/Matt Slocum, p. 7; © Panoramic Images/Getty Images, p. 8; © Kimberly Gatenby, p. 10; AP Photo/Reading Eagle, Susan L. Angstadt, p. 12; Tom "Mo" Moschella/Icon SMI 434/Newscom, pp. 14, 16; © Rich Pilling/Major League Baseball/Getty Images, p. 17; © George Gojkovich/Getty Images, p. 19; © Rob Leiter/Major League Baseball/Getty Images, p. 20; © Jamie Squire/Getty Images, p. 21; AP Photo/Rusty Kennedy, p. 22; AP Photo/Charles Krupa, p. 23; © Mitchell Layton/Getty Images, p. 24; © Doug Pensinger/Getty Images, pp. 25, 26; © Nick Laham/Getty Images, p. 27; © Mike McGinnis/Cal Sport Media/ZUMA Press, p. 28; © Jim McIsaac/Getty Images, p. 29.

Front cover: AP Photo/Bill Kostroun.

Main body text set in PMN Caecilia 16/28. Typeface provided by Linotype AG.